TEACHING KIDS TO WRITE WELL

....

Six Secrets Every Grown-up Should Know

TEACHING KIDS TO WRITE WELL

....

*Six Secrets Every Grown-up
Should Know*

Laurisa White Reyes

Skyrocket Press
SANTA CLARITA, CA

Copyright © 2015 by Laurisa White Reyes.

All rights reserved. No part of this publication may be reproduced, distributed or transmitted in any form or by any means, including photocopying, recording, or other electronic or mechanical methods, without the prior written permission of the publisher, except in the case of brief quotations embodied in critical reviews and certain other noncommercial uses permitted by copyright law. For permission requests, write to the publisher, addressed "Attention: Permissions Coordinator," at the address below.

Skyrocket Press
28020 Newbird Drive
Santa Clarita, CA 91350
www.skyrocketpress.com

First Edition published in 2009

Book Layout ©2013 BookDesignTemplates.com

ISBN: 978-0-9863924-7-4

Teaching Kids To Write Well: 6 Secrets Every Grown-up Should Know. – 2nd ed.

This book is dedicated to

Elizabeth Rose

ALSO BY LAURISA WHITE REYES

The Rock of Ivanore
The Last Enchanter
Contact
The Crystal Keeper: Exile
The Crystal Keeper: Betrayal
The Crystal Keeper: Vengeance

TABLE OF CONTENTS

Introduction: Why Writing Matters i
Part I: The 6 Secrets
    Secret #1: Let Them See You Write 1
    Secret #2: Teach the Rules 17
    Secret #3: Throw Away the Red Pen 29
    Secret #4: Turn Off the TV! 49
    Secret #5: Make Writing Fun 67
    Secret #6: Raise the Bar 85
Part II: The Mechanics of Learning
    The 7 Stages of a Writing Education 103
    Writing Strategies That Work 115
Conclusion 127
About the Author 129
Works Cited 131

INTRODUCTION

WHY WRITING MATTERS

This book is specifically about writing, but it is also generally about learning. In its pages, I discuss how to stop the negative attitudes about writing that are passed from one generation to another, negativity that stunts the imagination and shackles the human spirit. It is about how to let learning become an end unto itself, rather than a grade on a report card, and how to foster within your child a love of the written word as a means of expressing his deepest and fondest desires.

Writing is more than letters of the alphabet or words on a page. It is the second most important means by which humankind communicates with itself, the first being speech. Unfortunately, the English language, both verbal and written, is in decline. With the advent of email and text messaging, continued growth of the non-English-speaking population, and increased numbers of students who drop out of school, America is experiencing a dumbing down of language. SAT scores for the 2006 graduating high school class showed the largest year-to-year decline since 1975[1], and more recently in 2013, the College Board expressed concern over the low scores, stating that "roughly 6 in 10 college-bound high school students who took the test were so lacking in their reading, writing and math skills, they were unprepared for college-level work."[2] This persistent pattern of declining test scores has caused experts in the educational field to sound the alarm.

In generations past, an individual who could not communicate effectively with others was considered ignorant, uneducated, even unintelligent. Today, poor language skills are often considered trendy and are representative of the American teen culture. However, while it may

---

[1] Education Wonks
[2] Sanchez

be popular for young people to hardly finish a sentence or to text using nothing but acronyms, inadequate communication skills will eventually prove an obstacle in their lives.

In their report, *Because Writing Matters: Improving Student Writing in Our Schools*, The National Writing Project and author Carl Nagin state the following.

> "In today's business world, writing is a 'threshold skill' for both employment and promotion. In a 2004 survey of 120 major American corporations, respondents emphasized that people who cannot write and communicate clearly will not be hired and are unlikely to last long enough to be considered for promotion."[3]

In other words, in a time when jobs are already hard to come by (U.S. unemployment rates averaged around 7% in 2013), applicants lacking appropriate communication skills find it difficult to compete for those jobs.

In contrast, those who *do* speak and write well stand out in a crowd. They are confident in

---

[3] Nagin, 17

themselves, obtain higher levels of education, earn more money in the workforce, and often become the leaders in our society. According to the College Board's National Commission on Writing, two-thirds of salaried workers in large U.S. companies are required to write, yet over three billion dollars are spent annually in trying to improve employees' poor writing skills.

Good writing skills are also critical to academic success. A large number of exams given in colleges and universities require essays. But despite the importance of good writing skills in higher education and in the workplace, these skills are in decline.

This is actually good news for your children. If you are reading this book, you are concerned about your child or students' writing skills and are searching for a way to improve them. By setting your child on the path to writing more effectively, he will one day find himself in that ever-shrinking pool of qualified college and/or job applicants who rise, like cream, to the top. Even if your child chooses to remain outside the mainstream workforce by being an entrepreneur or a stay-at-home parent, excellent writing skills will always play a valuable role in his life.

Research cited in *Because Writing Matters* shows that writing helps develop thinking and problem-solving skills.[4] Additionally, utilizing writing in all academic subjects aids in the retention of knowledge and improves reading skills. According to the National Writing Project, "If students are to learn, they must write."[5]

The six secrets discussed in this book are not really secrets at all. Rather they are suggestions on how to create a positive writing environment in your home. Good writing demands an open mind and a positive attitude. Without them, writing becomes a chore, or worse, an assignment. While there is nothing wrong with writing assignments, there is something fundamentally distasteful about turning a child off to writing.

At the end of this book, you will find a guide to the various stages of learning to write, as well as a description of several teaching strategies to make your child's writing education a success. My intention is to help you, the parent and/or teacher, help your child discover the joy of writing. Once the door to good writing is flung open, all the barriers and blockades that trip up the rest of us will vanish for your child. He will become an "I

---

[4] Ibid, 22
[5] Ibid, 104

can" person, and the wonderful side effect is that, as his parent and/or teacher, you will, too.

PART 1: THE 6 SECRETS

SECRET #1

LET YOUR CHILD SEE *YOU* WRITE

"I talk and talk and talk, and I haven't taught people in fifty years what my father taught by example in one week." – Mario Cuomo

Let's be honest. After reading the title of this chapter, some of you want to set this book aside and walk away. You may be thinking, *Me? Write?* But bear with me here. If you read nothing else in this book, read this chapter.

Prior to my becoming a published author of several children's books, I spent eight years as a writing instructor for a homeschool co-op. One afternoon following one of my writing classes, I chatted with some of my students' mothers. I asked them why they enrolled their children in my class. All of these women were intelligent, mature, and confident, but they had one other thing in common: each had had a negative experience when they were children or teens that convinced them they could not write well.

One by one these women shared their stories. A teacher had criticized one in front of her class. Another had a teacher who covered her work in red marks. Still another was bored with the assignments given her.

Since then, I have discovered that a large number of adults have had similar experiences. As a result of these experiences, many parents feel unqualified to teach their children how to write beyond the ABC's and simple sentences. Yet if I were to ask these same parents if they were qualified to teach their child to walk, to talk, ride a bicycle, or even to read, they would answer with a resounding, *Yes! Of course!*

Learning to write may not be as simple a task as learning to walk or talk, but the process of learning is much the same. There are three basic stages of learning: *Discovery*, *Desire* and

Discipline. In order for adults to be effective teachers of writing, they must understand their role in helping their children develop through each of these stages.

Discovery

Do you remember the first time you wanted to walk? You were most likely between the ages of eight and fourteen months when you first pulled yourself up to a standing position and grinned proudly at your parents as if to say, "See, Mom? See what I just did?"

As your legs grew stronger and your balance increased, you took those first hesitant steps, "cruising" along from couch to coffee table, to chair to couch again. Finally, with your parents coaxing you with open arms, you gleefully pitter-pattered across the floor into their waiting embraces.

What was it that first moved you, an infant, to make that first attempt to stand on your own? Some would say it was instinct, like little birds fluttering their wings to take flight, and for the most part they are correct. But I contend that there was something more.

Human nature is driven toward progress. Even the little baby somehow knows he is meant to do more than eat, cry, and sleep for the rest of his life. Like walking, communication is something to which human beings are naturally inclined. Children learn to walk and to talk by *observing* other humans walk and talk. Mobility, language, and many other basic skills are developed not by active teaching, but through passive observation. At first the child mimics what he sees or what he hears without fully understanding if these actions have any meaning. Later, he begins to imitate the adults around him, those whom he respects and, hopefully, loves. He wants to be like them, so he does what they do.

A good example of this is when a young child picks up a book and "reads" it. Maybe she holds the book upside down. Maybe the story she recites bears no resemblance to what is actually printed inside, but that doesn't matter to her. What matters is that Mommy reads, and she wants to read, too.

When he was four years old, my third child came to me with a stack of papers in his hand. I had given him an old manuscript of mine to use for scratch paper. He took the manuscript and set up his dresser like a desk, with a penholder, a chair, and a supply of writing utensils. He spent hours sitting at his desk, scribbling on sheet after sheet of paper. When he was finished, he presented me with his collection of scribbles and announced it was his book. Needless to say, I was honored. Imitation is my favorite form of flattery.

Maybe instinct drove my son to learn to walk, but would he have known how to sit at a desk and write if he had not seen me do it first?

Children are naturally curious. They want to explore their world and learn all they can about it. As parents, we teach them how to color with crayons, how to brush their teeth, how to dress themselves. Children first learn that these behaviors exist by catching others in the act.

When it comes to writing, let your children catch you in the act. Emails, personal letters, grocery lists, calendars, poems, diary entries—whatever drives you to put pen to paper, make sure you do it where your children can observe you. It won't be long before they will be writing, too.

Desire

While children naturally imitate the behaviors and actions of those around them, eventually, as they grow a little older, they start to learn how to do things because they *want* to.

This desire first presents itself during the toddler years when the child's will conflicts with his parents' or siblings' wills. An older brother plays with a truck and the three-year-old wants that truck for himself. He grabs it, and a tug of war ensues.

At first glance, this situation appears undesirable. Good children, of course, should share. But these children are also learning something very important: they are learning that they have their own unique wants and needs, and that they have the power to satisfy them.

This is the very reason why, as frustrating as it is for us adults, we let our children dress themselves, tie their own shoes, make their beds, etc. Most of the time, it would simply be easier for us to do these things for them. The dishes would be cleaner, the house would be more organized, and our children would always be wearing matching socks. However, we would rob our children of the satisfaction of accomplishing something on their own.

Human nature demands that we pursue our own interests. We don't like other people making all our decisions for us. From a very early age, children stake out their own talents and hobbies and interests and dreams.

One little girl wants to be a nurse when she grows up. Another girl loves horses. A young boy is practically obsessed with baseball, while his brother dreams of being an astronaut. No one told these children what they should love or want to be when they grow up. They decided these things on their own.

When it comes to writing, and even reading, one of the biggest mistakes we make with our children is demanding that they read certain books or write on particular subjects with little regard to the child's interests.

Imagine for a moment that you receive notice from the local city council that you have to arrange your front lawn and garden the way they tell you to. They include a list of flowers you are required to plant and a diagram to show you how to arrange them.

How would you feel about that? What would you do? Some people might shrug their shoulders and follow instructions as outlined out of fear or from a desire to please their superiors.

Other people might feel angry. *How dare anyone tell me how to arrange my own yard?* They might obey the directive, but would do so reluctantly and resent the intrusion. Or they might rebel altogether, preferring to risk getting fined rather than submitting to what they consider to be a form of tyranny.

But the city council has its reasons for requiring everyone to plant the same garden. The city would look prettier, more organized and unified. Perhaps the state government is offering monetary incentives for implementing a beautification agenda. Rewards are given to those who comply. Punishments are assigned to those who don't.

What is wrong with this picture?

The creativity and freedom of the individual has been sacrificed for what is perceived to be the public good. Human beings resent being told what to do all the time. Joe wants to plant daisies in his yard. Bonnie likes roses. Mary wants a southwest look with cactus and sandstone. Maybe the city could provide guidelines suggesting certain types of plants that enhance the natural environment, but the final decisions should be left up to each individual property owner.

Shouldn't reading and writing be like this, too? Would you like it if you could only read what someone else told you to read? I could tell you to read Nathaniel Hawthorne's *The Scarlet Letter*. It is a very good book, and you might like it. But if you were forced to read it, how much would you really get out of it? You might end up resenting the teacher and hating the book.

That's what often happens in school. Students are told what they will read and what they will write. The teachers, of course, have the children's best interests at heart. It is for their own good that they read *Huckleberry Finn* or write an essay on the Revolutionary War. These things are important! They need to be learned!

There are a few students who, like the compliant gardeners, shrug their shoulders and do the assignment. They do what is asked of them so they can earn the reward that is offered: an 'A' on their report card. Maybe, if the teacher is lucky, one or two of these students might actually love the assigned topic. But the vast majority of students are less than enthused. Some resent it, but do it anyway, just to get a passing grade. Others rebel, preferring a bad grade to wasting their time on a topic that is of no interest to them.

Wouldn't it be nice if every child could love what she reads or feel enthusiastic about researching a topic and writing about it?

This is not an unrealistic expectation. The key to helping children enjoy writing is to tap into a child's natural *desire* to pursue his or her own interests.

A child who loves football will *want* to read about it, write a letter to his favorite player, or learn how to play football himself.

A girl who loves poetry will *want* to read poetry, write poetry, and learn what she needs to know to become a successful poet one day.

As a boy, my father loved comic books, but he couldn't read. That didn't stop him, however. Though he liked the pictures, he really wanted to know what the words said. Over time, through his love of comic books, my dad taught himself to read.

As adults, we should pay more attention to our children's interests and then use those interests to motivate our children to learn. Parents know their children better than anyone else and are better able to connect them to the very resources that will motivate learning. The primary objective should be the *interest itself*, whether it is rocket ships, rabbits, or racquetball. The act of reading and writing should be secondary.

For example, when my oldest daughter was young, she developed an interest in monkeys. We went to the zoo to visit the chimpanzee, orangutan, and gorilla exhibits. We read all we could about them while there. Afterwards, we decided to write about what we learned. My daughter was too young to write on her own, but as I asked her questions, she dictated her answers, and I wrote them down. We included pictures we had taken that day and a postcard of the chimp exhibit.

This experience not only enabled Carissa to learn about something that interested her first hand, but she also learned how to put her knowledge into words and how those words are then written down.

Parents are best equipped to tap into their child's unique interests and talents and to use those interests as a tool for teaching literacy. The child is, of course, learning to read and write, but he is having fun doing it and does not concern himself so much with those things as he does with *what* he is reading and writing *about*.

Discipline

As children grow older, they will need to understand that sometimes we must learn for the sake of learning. They may not love math, but they need to learn the times tables anyway. They may not have a natural interest in history, but it is important that they know the difference between the Revolutionary and the Civil Wars.

These are just examples, of course. As adults, we understand that there are some things in this world that are important to know. We also realize that there are some things we must do whether we want to do them or not. The laundry must be washed and folded. The lawn must be maintained. The bills must be paid. A child learns how to commit himself to even seemingly undesirable tasks by watching his parents' examples. If the parents procrastinate, complain, and fail to get the job done, then the child will likely do the same. However, when parents are committed and dependable, their children will learn the value of these qualities and will be more likely to develop them as well.

The difference between adults and children, however, is that adults generally understand *why* a thing must be done. We understand that even though we don't like mowing the lawn, if it doesn't get mowed, the grass will grow too long and make the yard look ugly. Unfortunately, adults sometimes forget to explain the *why* to their children. We tend to give a command, such as "Mow the lawn!" And when the child moans and asks, "But why?" we might respond with, "Because I said so!"

While knowing the *why* may not automatically make your children more committed right now, over time it will. Just as understanding the *why* of certain tasks is important, children should understand the *why* of learning to write well. What motivation is there in writing a five paragraph essay if the objective is nothing more than learning how to write a five paragraph essay? However, if the essay becomes a tool for learning something of interest to the student, then the motivation increases.

I taught a class in essay writing not long ago where my objective as the teacher was for my students to be able to create an outline, conduct research, and write a well-organized essay on a particular topic. I recalled having to write essays in high school and how much I dreaded them. So I decided to find some way for these students to learn what was necessary without turning them off to writing all together.

The answer was in allowing each student to choose a topic that was of great interest to him. The topics ranged from hamsters and alligator lizards to the history of baseball and how to play Yu-Gi-Oh. While I taught the very concrete skills they needed to write their essays, I allowed complete freedom in the subject matter.

On the last day of class, each student read his essay aloud. Not one student expressed boredom, frustration, or even apathy in their assignments. Rather, everyone was enthusiastic and proud of their accomplishments. Their primary objective of learning about something they loved was obtained, and my objective of teaching them how to write an essay was also obtained.

Children need to learn to write well, but unless there is some obvious benefit to them, they will resist learning it. I am not talking about unrelated incentives like candy or an allowance. I am talking about a desire to develop a skill that will enable them to pursue their interests.

If a child needs to improve his penmanship, have him write something that must be read by someone he cares about. Grandpa has to be able to read his letter, so he needs to write as neatly as possible.

If an older child needs to write a book report, have him choose a friend that he thinks would like to read it, too. Have him find some fun way to tell this friend about the book, such as creating a book cover, making a poster, or retelling the story in his own words.

If a teen needs to learn to write a bibliography, let him gather together some of his favorite books and practice on those.

When to Begin

Experts in the educational field have found that it is best to begin teaching children to write at an early age, and that reading and writing are "best learned together."[6]

Formal instruction may not commence until a child is six, seven, or even eight years old, but that does not mean a younger child cannot grasp the fundamental concepts of reading and writing.

Learning to read begins the first time a mother opens a picture book and reads it to her baby. Repeated daily interactions between parent, child, and books soon form the foundation that will one day motivate that child to learn to read on his own.

Likewise, when a child is introduced to words printed on a page, he is already gaining the preliminary understanding that letters form words, words form sentences, and these words and sentences express ideas.

---

[6] Ibid, 60

During recent decades there has been an increasing push for parents to read to their children. Research has shown that when parents and children read consistently together, literacy improves.

The same holds true with writing.

In their report *Because Writing Matters,* The National Writing Project makes the following observation: "We cannot build a nation of educated people who can communicate effectively without teachers and administrators who value, understand, and practice writing themselves."[7]

Might I suggest that we cannot build a nation of educated people without *parents* who value, understand, and practice writing themselves. Teachers and administrators may have the expertise and curricula to educate mass numbers of students in the more technical side of writing, but no teacher is more effective in instilling within a child the love of writing than a parent who loves that child and who teaches by example.

---

[7] Ibid, 60

SECRET # 2

TEACH THE RULES

"There must be deviations from the rules in order to express almost anything....However, only the man who is familiar with the rules may sometimes violate them, for he alone can know that, in certain cases, the rule is not enough."
– Andre Ernest Modeste Gretry

When I first began to teach writing classes, I went into the job with the assumption that my students already understood the basic rules of grammar and punctuation, and for the most part my assumption was correct. However, the most disconcerting discovery I made was that such an assumption could not be made about every child.

Mary's Story

Mary* was fourteen years old and what I would call a bookworm. She was an eager learner and highly intelligent. On the last day of my fiction writing course that year, each of my students were to bring a typed copy of their short story to share with the class.

Mary did not want to read her story out loud, so I volunteered to read it for her. When she handed me her story, however, I was flabbergasted to find not one single use of punctuation on the entire page. There wasn't a period, comma, or quotation mark in sight. Not only that, but not a single letter was capitalized, every fifth word was misspelled, and the story had been written in one very long block of text. No paragraphs. I did my best to read it, but I struggled to know where to begin and end each sentence.

My class was not a grammar class. I was teaching the craft of fiction writing and expected the kids to learn the basic tools of writing at home. In this case, however, that had obviously not occurred.

When I had the chance, I pulled Mary aside and complimented her on her creative story. She had a knack for humor and character development.

"But," I told her as gently as I possibly could, "there is no punctuation on the entire page."

"Oh, I don't need punctuation," was her confident reply.

The truth is I am still stunned that anyone could honestly believe they don't need to use punctuation when they write. I don't know if her mother had told her that or if she had come to that conclusion on her own, but she was wrong, and I told her so.

Mary's case was a bit extreme. The vast majority of students who have received any kind of writing instruction, whether at home or in a classroom, will have learned the value of punctuation, proper grammar, and spelling. But parents and teachers should not be lulled into the same easy assumption as I was and allow your child/student to get as far as high school without even being able to put a period in the right place.

Society often tells us, though flippantly, that rules are made to be broken. Writers and poets in particular are notorious for breaking rules.

In his Pulitzer Prize winning memoir *Angela's Ashes*, author Frank McCourt avoids punctuation marks like the plague. Ernest Hemingway's original works were littered with misspelled words. William Faulkner was notorious for his run-on sentences.

This bending and breaking of the rules in contemporary literature may give young writers the impression that the rules are irrelevant when compared to the creative process of writing. This could not be further from the truth. Rules of writing should not be broken, must not be broken, until they are first mastered. If Frank McCourt had written a quotation mark-free story for his college professor, he probably would have received a poor grade indeed.

Mary's comment that she did not need to use punctuation is to writing like saying we do not need to obey traffic signals is to driving a vehicle. If we fail to stop at a red light, for example, cars will crash into each other, causing a lot of chaos and damage. The same thing happens to language without the proper use of punctuation and grammar.

In Mary's case, my opportunities to assist her were limited. However, I did manage to teach her a few simple self-checks to help her get her writing under control, which I will explain further in the next section of this book.

Teaching the Basics

It is easier to form good habits than to break bad ones. Teach grammar. Teach punctuation. Teach spelling. From early on, encourage a child to correct his own work, with your supervision, of course. He will become confident not only in his ability to write, but also in his ability to see mistakes and correct them.

I am often asked what curriculum should be used for teaching children the basics and what is the best method for teaching them, to which I really do not have a pat answer. There must be hundreds of spelling and grammar workbooks available these days. However, I tend to shy away from what I call busywork, endless worksheets with blank lines. While worksheets might be fine for some kids, for others they are a certain invitation to boredom, and boredom is the antithesis of learning.

Learning can only take place when the child feels enthused about what he is learning. Otherwise the information will most likely be forgotten. So, how do you get your child enthused about grammar and punctuation?

A good place to start is with reading. When you read to your young child, does he "read" along with you? If so, once in a while point out the periods and the question marks. Explain what they are and how they work. Have him point out others that he sees in the story. Once a child learns to recognize the letters of the alphabet, have him point out words that start with certain letters.

Games are a wonderful way to help children remember the rules of writing. There are many from which to choose including *Word Bingo*, *Scrabble*, *Learning Wrap-Ups* and *Grammar Puzzles*. A Google search for grammar games, parts of speech, and other related topics turns up dozens of websites that offer free online games to reinforce what children learn.

The point is to make learning fun. A child who is involved with the story his mother is reading may not realize he is learning, but he is just the same.

In the Beginning

For children who can read independently, I like to print out word cards, preferably on blank index cards. Each part of speech is a different color:

> nouns – dark blue
> verbs – dark green

adjectives – light blue
adverbs – light green
articles – black
conjunctions – orange
prepositions – purple

I introduce the articles (the, a, an), nouns, and verbs first and explain that all sentences need a noun and a verb. The students can arrange the cards in different patterns to make sentences. Later on, I add adjectives, adverbs, conjunctions, and prepositions, giving plenty of time in between for the student to experiment with arranging their cards.

The best way for kids to remember what they learn is to allow them to make funny, even nonsensical sentences such as: **The purple dog burps loudly.**

I also introduce *Magic S*. *Magic S* must appear in all sentences either at the end of a noun – if it is plural—or at the end of the verb—if it is singular. (This applies to present tense.) I also explain that sometimes *Magic S* has to have an 'e' in front of it, such as with **dishes** or **classes**.

Any basic grammar workbook will contain the lessons needed to teach a younger child the tools for constructing words and sentences. The point is to make learning them enjoyable.

Let me point out, however, that rules of grammar are best learned through language. A child first learns to speak English. Then he learns to write it. In teaching writing, we need to explain the correlation between sound and the symbols written on a page. For example, we might write the letter **A** on a piece of paper. Then we tell our child, "This is an **A**. It sounds like ă."

This makes no sense to a young child until we use the sound in the context of words that are familiar to him: "**Ă** like *apple.*"

Suddenly, a light goes on. This sound ă has a written symbol '**A**', as do all the sounds in our language. Grammar works very much the same way. Children are not *taught* to speak in sentences. They learn by listening to others speak. Then they try it out on their own, first sounds, then words, and finally sentences. A three-year-old has no idea what a subject or a predicate is. They don't know the difference between nouns and verbs. And yet they use these parts of speech to speak in sentences.

We adults need only to teach our children to write the way they speak. When a six-year-old says, "That puppy is cute!" encourage him to write those words in a journal or a letter to Grandma. In fact, having the child say his thoughts out loud before he writes is always a good idea. If it sounds right coming out of his mouth, (and even children can sense when a sentence works or doesn't work) then what he writes will likely be right, too.

Below is a dialogue between a child and his mother about *Magic S*. See how the mother uses what already comes naturally to her son to teach him an important rule of grammar.

Mom: Billy, do you know what letter this is?
Billy: That's an '**S**'! It sounds like *ssss*.
Mom: Very good. This is *Magic S*. *Magic S* is very special. When you put it on the end of a word, you can change that word. Billy, if you went to the pet store to buy food for your cat, the salesperson might ask you how many cats you have. What would you tell him?
Billy: I have one cat.
Mom: Okay. Let's write the word cat. C-A-T. Very nice. Now, what if you have more than one cat? Maybe you have three or four? What would you tell the salesman then?
Billy: I have three cats
Mom: Do you hear a difference? One cat. Three cats.

Billy: There is an '**s**' at the end of one of them.

Mom: That's right. That's the *Magic S* I was telling you about. At first you only had one cat. But now let's write '**S**' at the end of your word C-A-T. Now what does it say?

Billy: Cats!

Mom: When you add *Magic S* to the end of a word, it changes it from only one to more than one! Pretty neat, right?

Billy: Yeah! Can I add *Magic S* on some other words?

Mom: Sure, Billy. Let's try the word hat…

As you can see, Billy already knew how to use *Magic S* in his speech. He learned the rule when he learned to talk. His mother simply explained how the rule works and how to write it down. This same method can be used for any rule, even more complex rules, as I will now explain.

Teaching Older Children

The above example was a dialogue between a mother and a five or six-year-old child. But what if you are teaching a ten, twelve, or fourteen-year-old?

As your child gets older, the rules become more complex, but your system for teaching them does not. This is because the older a child becomes, the more sophisticated his speech will be. Once again, older children instinctively know the rules, even if they are not yet able to explain them.

For example, if you were to teach your child about compound sentences, you would begin by having a natural dialogue with your child. If you listen closely, you will notice that he uses compound sentences quite often. We all do.

"I went to the mall, and I bought a denim jacket. It cost twenty dollars, but I didn't have enough. So I borrowed some from Jane."

Here is a prime opportunity for a teaching moment. First, point out that "I went to the mall" contains all the elements essential to a sentence. It could stand alone, all by itself. So could "I bought a denim jacket."

Your child will nod his head. This is simple stuff. He already knows that. Then you might point out that he linked the two sentences together with the word *and*. He took two sentences and made them into one compound sentence. Tell him he can do this by using contractions: *and*, *but*, and *or*.

This lesson would take all of one minute to learn. Now he will be conscious of this rule when he speaks and will be more likely to use it in his writing. This same technique can be used to teach proper punctuation, parts of speech, verb tenses, possessives, etc. The rules are easy to learn, but once your child is aware of the rules, he must be given ample opportunity to practice them IN WRITING. The section of this book entitled *Secret #5: Make writing fun* lists creative ways to get your child to practice writing.

SECRET # 3

THROW AWAY THE RED PEN

"Children have more need of models than of critics." – Joseph Joubert

Tenth grade was not a good year for me. I was what some kids call *invisible*. Shy and awkward, I was doubly cursed with freckles and glasses. Needless to say, my self-esteem was nearly non-existent. The one thing about myself that I was proud of was my writing.

I began writing when I was just five years old. One night, I climbed out of bed and scavenged a piece of poster board from the trash whereon I scrawled my first poem:

> Candy, candy, what do you do?
> I give children toothaches and cavities, too.
> Candy, candy, why do you do?
> 'Cause I'm mean, mean, mean*!*

All right, so it isn't Shakespeare, but those words set me on a lifelong path that would eventually lead to a career as a writer.

As a child, I wrote poetry, plays, short stories, and songs, often blackmailing my brothers and cousins into performing them for our parents. By the time I got to high school I thought I was pretty good at it … until I met Ms. Danson.*

My Story

Ms. Danson was a tall, imposing woman who looked more like a football player than a school teacher. She prided herself on the fact that she knew every spot on campus where students could ditch class and hide. She should know because she had graduated from our school only a few years earlier. This was her first teaching job, and I was unlucky enough to get her for English that year.

Now, as a student I was not anything special. However, I excelled at English. The only thing I loved more than writing was reading. I had fallen in love with literature during my freshman year thanks to Thelma Chapman, a vivacious English teacher with a delightful British accent. Due to my nearsightedness and my love of English, I always sat in the front row, but Ms. Danson seated her class alphabetically, and since I was the only "W" in class, I was relegated to the corner seat in the last row.

Our reading assignments that year included *The Adventures of Huckleberry Finn*. I was sure Mark Twain himself would have slept through Ms. Danson's lectures. To make matters even worse, we were to write a term paper on it. I was pretty good at poems and stories, but I wasn't so good at term papers. I did my best, however, and turned it in.

One afternoon toward the end of the second semester, Ms. Danson called me into her office. She slid my paper across her desk and instructed me to open the cover. I did so and found a big '**D-**' scrawled in red ink on the title page. Ms. Danson proceeded to flip through the pages, detailing all the mistakes I had made, from the lack of transitional phrases to putting my commas on the outside of my quotation marks. Red marks adorned every page. All I saw was red, and that

'**D-**' seared itself into my brain like a branding iron.

Then I did something that took Ms. Danson by surprise. I started to cry. I put my head down on her desk and wept like heartbroken child. Up until that moment, I had wanted nothing more than to grow up and become a famous best-selling author. It was my life's dream, and now that dream was shattered. Though Ms. Danson had not said the actual words, what all those red marks told me was that I was a failure. It was a devastating discovery.

Perhaps if my experiences with writing had ended there, I might never have picked up a pen again. Fortunately, tenth grade ended, and the next year I was assigned to Elizabeth Rose for English.

I had heard rumors about Mrs. Rose, that she was a bit unusual, and perhaps she was. She was a tiny woman with long, straight platinum blonde hair. She wore high heels, short skirts, and a lot of make-up. She was animated, moving her hands and head when she talked so that her hair bobbed up and down against her shoulders. But her most distinctive feature was how much she loved teaching. It was evident in everything she said and did. Red marks on student assignments were few and far between. Instead, she covered her students' papers with rubber stamped images—she had hundreds of rubber stamps in her collection.

When Mrs. Rose read a story, the words jumped right off the page. I would often sit with my elbows on my desk and my chin propped in the palms of my hands, listening to her read *Rebecca*, *Gone With The Wind*, or *The Haunting of Hill House*. I fell in love with literature all over again that year, and thanks to Mrs. Rose, I picked up that pen and started to write again.

Unlike Ms. Danson who focused on mistakes, Mrs. Rose accentuated the positive, encouraging her students to see their own potential. Instead of a term paper, she put us in groups and told us to write "Gone With the Wind: 10 Years Later." She told me I had talent, that I was a writer at heart and should pursue my dream. Now, having spent two decades as a professional writer, I am living that dream every day.

What made the difference for me? The answer is simple. Someone believed in me. Someone took the time to focus on my positives and let the negatives take care of themselves. I wasn't a perfect student, but Mrs. Rose saw potential where Ms. Danson saw flaws. In time, I learned how to use punctuation correctly and how to write a proper bibliography. More importantly, I learned how to organize my thoughts and put them on paper. That would never have happened if all I ever saw was red.

The "I Can" Attitude

The most common remark I hear from my students' parents is, "I can't write." That is often the very reason why they enroll their children in my classes. They lack the confidence to teach their children to write because they lack confidence in their own ability to write. From speaking with many of them, I have discovered that their experiences in school were not unlike my own. Unfortunately, most of them did not have a Mrs. Rose to rectify the situation. They grew up believing that writing well is something only talented people do, as if writing was some divine gift magically bestowed on some and not others.

This simply isn't the case. I don't know of a single talented person who did not work hard to learn how to do whatever it is they do. Painters, musicians, designers, writers—all had to learn their craft. They took classes, studied, were mentored, and practiced, practiced, practiced until they could make it look easy. Other people call them talented, but the true artist knows how hard he had to work to get there.

I believe that anyone can be "talented" if they are willing to do what it takes to learn whatever it is they want to learn. However, one tremendous obstacle blocks the path of creativity for far too many people today. It is as inconspicuous as a small stone in their paths, yet as difficult as a mountain to remove. This is the devastating "I can't" attitude that afflicts our society today.

Where does this negative attitude, this false doctrine of the human existence, come from?

I may be stoned for saying this, but I believe it comes from the way we teach our children. The way *we* were taught. The way our parents were taught. In school, children are given only two options: pass or fail. Let me explain what I mean.

The '**A**' stamped at the top of students' papers represents an elusive perfection that all are expected to achieve, yet few do. Anything other than an '**A**' means they have fallen short of perfection, and have therefore failed.

Too many teachers look for mistakes in their students' work. The focus is on what has *not* been learned, the answers that are not correct. Red marks highlight flaws and imperfections, and report cards make kids feel inadequate and ashamed of themselves. Knowledge is translated into a GPA, numbers: 4.0, 3.4, 2.1, and so forth. The knowledge itself is, for the most part, forgotten because it was never really learned in the first place. Instead of being integrated into a student's mind and being, facts are regurgitated to please the teacher and the parent. The objective is to get the grade, not to learn.

As a result, many students come away from school with neither the grades nor the education that we adults hope they would acquire. Instead of feeling passionate about learning, too many young people become convinced that they *can't*. They *can't* play volleyball, they *can't* remember history, they *can't* do Algebra, they *can't* write.

All these *cant*'s. Where are the *can*s? How many students leave public school enthusiastic about something, anything? How many say "*I can?*"

It All Begins with Attitude

In his best-selling book, *Learned Optimism: How to Change Your Mind and Your Life*, author Martin E. P. Seligman, Ph. D. discusses the development of self-talk in children, something he calls their *explanatory style*. He states that a child's opinion of himself and the way he talks himself through difficult situations has a great deal to do with how the adults in his life respond to negative situations.

For example, if a mother responds with anger at getting a small dent in her car, blaming it on her own or someone else's stupidity, the child will learn to respond the same way. His perception of the world and his role in it is largely shaped by what his mother's words and behavior reveals about her own self-perception.

"Children's antennae are constantly tuned to the way their parents, particularly their mothers, talk about causes of emotionally loaded events," observes Dr. Seligman. "It is no accident that 'Why?' is one of the first and most repeated questions that young children ask...Your children hang on every word of the explanations you give, particularly when something goes wrong."[8]

In the area of academics, including learning to write well, a mother's (or teacher's) response to her child's imperfections and mistakes has an enormous influence on his self-esteem, as well as his overall attitude about life. When a child brings home a low score on a spelling test, and his

---

[8] Seligman, 128

mother scolds him for it or calls him stupid, he will develop a pessimistic attitude. He will learn that mistakes are absolute, and that he cannot do any better. Dr. Seligman reminds us that, "children believe the criticisms they get, and use them to form their explanatory style."[9]

In contrast, when mistakes are recognized for what they are—mistakes—independent of the child's value and capabilities as a person, the child learns to see the world from an optimistic, less rigid point of view.

This is not to say that parents ought never to criticize their children. When criticism is given, it should be focused on the error rather than the child. However, never offering constructive criticism can be just as detrimental to a child as having a parent who is overly critical.

In their book, *The 7 Worst Things Good Parents Do*, authors John C. Friel and Linda D. Friel note that in trying to avoid hurting their children's feelings, some parents fail to give criticism even when it is necessary, robbing them of the very challenges that would eventually build character and self-esteem:

---

[9] Ibid, 129

"Of course we need to praise our children when they do things well. But we also need to let them struggle with problems by themselves and sometimes get their reward from the fact that they solved a problem on their own. We need to teach our kids about life. It isn't enough to pump them up with empty praise for a job poorly done. We need to guide, teach, gently correct and help our kids move toward competence. Self-esteem, after all, comes from competence, not from incompetence…Our job as parents is to help our children discover their own gifts and then learn to do them well."[10]

We will discuss the concept of struggle further in *Secret # 6: Raise The Bar*. For the time being, however, it is vital that we understand how debilitating negativity and pessimism can be. Studies have found that even the most talented children, if their attitude is negative, often do poorly in school. In adulthood, pessimism contributes to general unhappiness and depression. On the other hand, optimism, *not talent*, appears to be the primary factor behind academic success and overall satisfaction with life. The Friels tell us that

---

[10] Friel, 14-15

"talent is overrated." In their research, they have found that pessimists consistently "drop below their 'potential', and optimists exceed it."[11] The good news is, however, that "if children can learn [pessimism], they can unlearn it...."[12]

Taking Ownership

One way to help a child develop optimism is to allow him ownership of his own accomplishments *and mistakes*. This *is not* what generally occurs in most school settings. When a child completes an assignment in school, the teacher corrects the assignment. She marks up the page with a red pen and tells the child everything that he did wrong.

This system of correcting assignments may work for grading math tests, but it can backfire when used on written composition.

First of all, writing is a creative process. In putting words on paper to express thoughts and ideas, the student has in fact placed a little piece of himself on that paper. He takes pride in his creation, much as he would as if he had painted a picture.

---

[11] Ibid, 154
[12] Ibid, 235

Imagine if your six-year-old came to you with a crayon drawing he made. As parents, we would never criticize him for coloring out of the lines or for using the wrong colors. Instead, we praise him. We tell him what a good job he's done. We know that as he gets older, his coordination will increase and his skills will improve.

As with art, children ought to experiment with words long before we ever even think about correcting their work. When they grow older, we may think it is okay now to criticize and point out flaws. But the truth is that hearts are still sensitive and egos easily bruised. Adults are no different than children in this aspect. How would you feel if you had spent time writing a letter or drawing a picture and someone took a red pen and wrote all over it telling you everything you did wrong? Would you want to do it again?

It isn't that corrections should not be made. However, *the one making the corrections should be the student, not the teacher.*

For example, my son struggled with writing in the fourth grade. Among his difficulties was his tendency to forget to capitalize the first letter of his sentences. I could have easily grabbed a red pen and circled all the mistakes in his assignments, and that's just what I did at first.

I noticed that he became frustrated whenever he had to write an assignment. He took every correction as a personal insult. It was as though I were criticizing *him* rather than the work.

I decided to try something different. Instead of me pointing out his mistakes, I reminded him, in a pleasant tone of voice, of the rule of capitalization. Then I asked him to read his paper to see if there were any words he needed to capitalize.

His discoveries resulted in a little embarrassed laughter and a prompt correction. The rule was reinforced, and his pride was left intact. He now remembers more often than not to capitalize the first letters in his sentences, and the moaning and groaning over writing assignments, while still present, is slowly disappearing.

Allowing students to take ownership of their own work—including their mistakes—makes for more responsible and happy children. Learning to write well is a process, not a destination. Once children understand that the goal is progress rather than perfection, they soon learn that mistakes can be corrected and that they are fully capable of completing whatever assignment comes their way. Pessimism and self-doubt are replaced with an "I can" attitude.

The Value of Self Correcting

In the previous chapter, I shared the story of Mary, a fourteen-year-old girl who had difficulty with the basic rules of writing. It would have been easy for me to mark up her story and make the corrections for her, but it is better to place the responsibility of correcting one's work on the child's shoulders. Let the child *own* his or her own writing, mistakes and all.

Mary already knew the rules of writing but had chosen not to follow them. At fourteen-years-old, she would soon be thinking about attending college and looking for a job. I explained to her that she would need to write well to be accepted into college. If she were to write a college entry essay with no punctuation, she would be denied admittance every time. Even the most basic job applications require the ability to write.

Once she understood the importance of the rules, I had her read her story out loud. I asked her to do three things. First, every time she came to the end of a sentence she was to add a period. The voice naturally pauses at the ends of sentences, and I explained to Mary that punctuation is a written symbol of the pauses and fluctuations that occur naturally in speech, just as the letters of the alphabet represent the sounds of speech.

Next, Mary was to capitalize the first letter of every sentence. Once the periods were in place, it was much easier to locate the beginnings of the sentences. She also circled all the proper names on the page and capitalized those as well.

Finally, she read it out loud once more and underlined any word that she knew was misspelled. There were quite a few, and she found most of them on her own. We reviewed how to use a dictionary, and I assisted her in looking up the first three or four words. She then looked up the rest herself and wrote the correct spellings on her page.

As it turned out, she was relying solely on her computer spell check, which is handy for obvious words, but the longer words were spelled so strangely that the computer did not recognize them and therefore could not offer the correct spelling.

Spell check makes for lazy spellers. I recommend keeping a dictionary beside the computer at all times. When the spell check highlights a misspelled word, look it up in the dictionary. Your student's spelling will vastly improve this way.

Below, I have listed nine keys for helping children take ownership of their own work and develop an optimistic attitude toward writing.

#1: Teach the Rules. No one can master the rules of grammar if they do not know them. Teach your child to capitalize the first letter in a sentence and in proper names, put a period at the end of a sentence, use quotation marks around a direct quote, use parts of speech correctly, and so forth.

#2: Focus on Writing. Once the rules have been taught, turn your attention to the process rather than the rules of writing. For example, once you have explained to an art student the proper use of his brushes, you teach him to paint. You don't continually harp on the brushes.

#3: Allow For Mistakes. Your child will make mistakes, and that is okay. Let him complete his writing draft without correcting anything for him. Let him misspell as many words and leave out as many periods as he likes. Resist the urge to point out the errors.

#4: Listen. It is important that we recognize that children will likely have objections to assignments. Instead of demanding they complete an assignment (which quickly leads to anger and resentment), listen to what they have to say about it. Perhaps their objections are their way of telling you that they don't understand your instructions or that they need help.

#5: Ask Questions. Listening is good, but unless you respond to your child's comments in some way, he will still feel frustrated. Rephrase what he has said. Ask him if you have understood him correctly. Ask any further questions needed to clarify misunderstandings.

#6: Review the Rules. Discuss what your child knows about punctuation, grammar, and spelling. Be sure he fully understands how to use a dictionary, punctuation, correct grammar, spelling, etc. Emphasize those rules that you know are difficult for him.

#7: Read Out Loud. Have your child read his own writing to you out loud. As he reads, have him look for and correct his own mistakes. He will learn far more by editing and revising his own work than by you doing it for him. With practice he will soon be able to spot more errors, or even prevent making them.

#8: Give Constructive Feedback. Do not criticize or scold your child for his mistakes. However, when you see a weakness in his writing or errors that keep repeating themselves, point them out to him. Be sure to emphasize the mistake, not the child. Be patient and speak in a kind tone of voice. Reassure him that you are available to help him if needed.

#9: Give Honest Praise. Tell your child how proud you are of his efforts. Express confidence that he can write well and will improve with practice. Be specific when giving compliments, such as mentioning a particularly nice line of poetry, or remembering to use punctuation correctly. Consider displaying his writing where everyone in the family can see it.

SECRET # 4

TURN OFF THE TV!

"I have never seen a bad television program, because I refuse to. God gave me a mind, and a wrist that turns things off." – Jack Paar

According to the American Academy of Pediatrics, America's children watch an average of four hours of television each day. "In a year," says the Nemours Foundation, "the average child spends 900 hours in school and nearly 1,023 hours in front of a TV."[13]

Most adults are familiar with the risks to children of extended exposure to television. Over

---

[13] KidsHealth

four thousand studies conducted on the effects of television have found that too much television contributes to obesity, violent behavior, trauma, fear, and a warped sense of reality. These findings ought to be enough motivation for parents to curb the amount of TV time in their homes, but the fact that 99% of American households own a TV (66% own 3 or more) and that the average adult spends more than six hours a day watching television[14] reveals the sad truth that most parents really don't care.

What does all this have to do with writing well? A great deal, actually. One of the devastating effects of too much TV is that young minds are fed a constant diet of flashy images and manipulative storylines that have a very tangible detrimental effect on the development of cognitive processes.

The Death of Imagination

Dr. Jane Healy, author of *Endangered Minds: Why Children Don't Think and What We Can Do About It*, points out that environment has a physical effect on the developing human mind. As a child

---

[14] Herr

experiences life, everything he sees, hears, touches and tastes builds connections between synapses within the brain. The more varied his environment and the more input he receives, the more connections, or networks, are made. This process is how children learn language, develop fine motor skills, and become self-aware. These neuro-networks become permanent highways of information, and the highways that are most often used become the strongest while those that lack sufficient stimuli will die. It is a simple matter of *use it or lose it*.

"The experiences with which a child chooses to interact," says Dr. Healy, "determine each brain's synaptic structure as well as the way it functions for different types of learning...A healthy brain stimulates itself by active interaction with what it finds challenging and interesting in its environment."[15]

While television in and of itself is not inherently good or bad, its negatives can easily outweigh its positives. For example, the development of language and communication in today's children has been profoundly affected by their exposure to television. Dr. Jane Holmes

---

[15] Healy, 81-82

Bernstein, as quoted in *Endangered Minds*, says the following:

> "There's nothing wrong with TV or computers per se. However, it may be an issue whether the kids are active or passive when working with machines. *Sesame Street*, for example, has brought a great deal of information to children who might not otherwise have got it, but this may have been obtained at a price. I hear many teachers complain that children in kindergarten and first grade don't know how to listen actively! They're used to fast-paced segments of information that are constantly changing. They should be doing something with what they're getting. The *Sesame Street* population is actually at the greatest risk for not understanding that language is communication, a back and forth interaction between people. They aren't personally involved in using language to think and solve problems with. Children who have been talked to and had stories read to them are at a real advantage. They've learned how to listen and pay attention—and had fun doing it."[16]

---

[16] Ibid, 80

To reiterate, language is "a back and forth interaction between people."[17] Children need time away from the TV in order to learn how to utilize communication effectively.

Living TV Free

In 1997, my family was pretty much a mainstream TV-addicted family. My kids watched *Barney* and *Sesame Street* every morning, I spent my days watching the *TV Food Network*, and evenings were spent glued to *Friends*, *Frazier*, and many other shows that everyone who was anyone at the time watched. As devout Christians and parents of two small children, my husband and I experienced some discomfort with the fact that behaviors we would never condone in ourselves or in our children (such as sexual promiscuity, violence, etc.) were our primary source of entertainment. However, TV for us was as much a part of our lives as eating, sleeping or breathing—just as it still is for the vast majority of Americans, so turning it off was simply not an option.

---

[17] Ibid, 80

Yet something kept nagging at the back of my brain. I often watched morning cartoons with my kids and was amazed at how inane and, quite frankly, stupid most shows were. Hours were wasted on watching grown men sing silly songs or puppets "talk" to my kids in a manner I considered condescending. What was called educational TV was, in actuality, nothing more than free babysitting.

The situation was even worse for us grown-ups. My husband would come home from a long day at work and plop down on the sofa to watch the news. The same news stories ran over and over and over, yet the TV stayed on. Conversation in our home was non-existent. At night, we rushed to put the kids to bed so we wouldn't miss the opening of the next episode of *X-Files*. And if the kids came into the living room to ask for a glass of water or another goodnight kiss, we would scream at them. "Be quiet! I can't hear the show!" They had to wait until the commercial to get whatever it was they wanted.

But it wasn't until the airing of an episode on *Ellen*, a popular sitcom at the time, that finally woke us up to the seriousness of our situation. On this particular episode, Ellen was going to kiss another woman. It was something I simply did not doing homework. An average of four hours are spent watching television (or other TV related activities such as video games.) Factor in time for eating, bathing and dressing, and you're left with maybe three hours of playtime—and often that time is eaten up by music lessons, scouting, church activities, sports practice, etc. Today's kids just don't have much spare time on their hands.

Until the advent of television in the mid-twentieth century, children played. They sang songs, skipped rope, played hopscotch, marbles, and baseball. They entertained themselves with hoola-hoops, slinkies, rubberband shooters, yo-yos, and anything else they could get their hands on. And they had plenty of time to do it.

Even kids who worked went home at the end of the day and played with their brothers and sisters or other neighborhood kids. Today, too many young people come home and just flip on the boob tube.

You might ask, what's wrong with that? The answer, of course, depends on what expectations you have for your child. If you want your child to accept what TV dishes out to him without question, then the answer is nothing. But if you're a parent who expects more out of life for your child, who wants your child to think for himself and to reach his fullest potential, then maybe it is time to think about cutting TV out of your life for good.

In his groundbreaking book *Dumbing Us Down: The Hidden Curriculum of Compulsory Schooling*, author John Taylor Gatto, a public school teacher for 30 years, says the following:

> "Two institutions at present control our children's lives: television and schooling, in that order. Both of these reduce the real world of wisdom, fortitude, temperance, and justice to a never-ending, nonstop abstraction…It's a simple matter of arithmetic: between schooling and television, all the time the children have is eaten up…Right now we are taking from our children all the time that they need to develop self-knowledge. That has to stop…But I am confident that as they gain self-knowledge they'll also become self-teachers—and only self-teaching has any lasting value. We've got to give kids independent time right away because that is the key to self-knowledge, and we must reinvolve them with the real world as fast as possible so that their independent time can be spent on something other than

abstraction. This is an emergency—it requires drastic action to correct."[18]

Mr. Gatto's observations are even more pressing today than they were when he made them in 1992. Children need time away from institutionalized entertainment and education so that they can have more self-teaching experiences. This is not to say that there are no redeeming programs on television and that video games should be avoided like the plague, but these activities, if not removed from the home altogether, should be enjoyed in moderation. In 2006, after many years of resistance, I finally broke down and bought a Play Station. Since then, we've upgraded to a PS2 and PS3, but the layer of dust on our current gaming system is a testament to how little it is played.

Some families prefer limiting the amount of time their children spend in front of the TV. It is up to you, as parents, to set such limits, but don't be fooled. Television is similar to narcotics in that once a little gets in your system, you'll need more and more to get your fix. Unlike narcotics,

---

[18] Gatto, 25 & 32

however, there are no withdrawal symptoms for going cold turkey.

Filling the Hole

So, with TV gone you suddenly have four hours extra time to fill. What now?

Every summer I take my kids to the beach. One of their favorite activities is to dig a hole in the sand as fast as they can before a wave comes to wash it away. If you have ever dug a hole in wet sand near the water's edge, then you have seen how the hole fills from the bottom up. The water level rises faster than you can scoop it out. Time is like that, too. After shutting off the TV, you might wander aimlessly about the house for a day or two looking for things to fill your time, but likely not. If anything, you will quickly discover how little time you really have and wonder how you could ever have wasted so much of it.

For children whose minds need time to develop and explore, resist the urge to fill that hole for them. It is a great temptation for parents today. There are so many worthwhile activities to keep kids busy, but is it busy-ness they need or authentic self-teaching experiences? I can assure you that your child will grow at the same rate and will have the same shot at becoming a self-sufficient, reasonably intelligent adult whether he plays city league football, joins the chess club, takes piano lessons, becomes a Boy Scout—or not. I am not suggesting that these activities and many others like them are bad, or even that all extracurricular activities should be avoided. However, it is vital that kids have time—unscheduled time—to do whatever they want, whether to write a poem, read a book, shoot hoops in the back yard, hang out with a friend, or do nothing at all.

However you decide to spend those extra hours a day, remember that your child needs to spend at least some of it alone. It is in those quiet moments when we are completely alone (no iPod, no video games, no nothing) that we are able to reflect on our lives. Many writers will tell you that a large chunk of their work is done inside their minds while they are *thinking*. Most adults do that. When problems arise at home or at work, grown-ups use those few precious moments alone to think them through. Kids need time to do the same. It is during the alone times in his day that he will be able to ponder on his writing, among other things. The imagination flourishes in solitude. Noise and busy-ness suffocate it.

The Value of Talk

Next to having alone time, the next best thing a child can do with his time is to spend it conversing with other people. According to Dr. Healy, one of the most important activities in which a child should participate is *talk*.

I am ashamed to admit this, but like far too many parents today, I often tell my kids to *be quiet*. But being quiet has the ugly result of numbing a child's natural craving for human interaction. Interactive talk between child and adult is vital to the healthy developing mind.

What kind of *talk* do we mean? There are several forms of communication that fall under the category of talk. When a parent reads a story out loud to her child and allows that child to ask questions and participate in other ways as well, that is talk.

Normal every day conversation around the dinner table, in the car, before bed—parents asking children what they did that day at school and then listening to their response—that is talk.

It is also important to understand what talk *is not*. Music piped directly into the ears via headphones, staring wide-eyed for hours at a television screen, single-player video games—

these activities do not require any interaction on the part of the listener, watcher or player, but instead isolate children from their environment and dull the mind's otherwise instinctive drive to come into physical and mental contact with it.

Talking does not have to be scheduled, forced, or planned. Very often it just happens, and parents who resist the urge to tell their kids to be quiet all the time and instead nurture their curiosity and creativity will, in the end, have children who are more independent and better able to understand and interact with their environment than those who are fed a steady dose of scripted monologue.

Reading vs. Television

The one "isolating" activity that is actually good for the developing brain is reading. While television requires little or no active participation on the part of the viewer, reading demands it.

Television and reading make very different demands on the human brain. TV is believed to reduce stimulation to the brain and its development of critical and analytical thinking, while reading has been proven to increase it.

Dr. Healy calls television's anesthetic affect on the brain "the Zombie effect" or "attentional inertia."

"The longer a look at TV continues, the greater the probability it will be maintained," observes Dr. Healy. "For example, if a child gets 'glued' to the set during a program, the more likely he is to remain fixated when the scene breaks into commercial. Mothers who have trouble summoning their children to chores, homework, or even supper are already aware that the longer a child has been watching TV, the slower he is to respond when someone calls his name."[19]

Unfortunately, this is the very reason why so many adults allow their children so much television time. It keeps the kids quiet, giving adults more time to do what they want to do without being interrupted.

I have five children, and there are times when I really, really want to be left alone. I can't even take a shower without someone walking in to the bathroom to ask me questions or make demands. (For some reason, they don't do this to my husband. I wonder why?) I often feel resentful of

---

[19] Healy, 204

the constant intrusion on my privacy and long for even an hour or two of absolute peace and quiet.

Our family has a rather substantial collection of videos, and there are days when, to preserve my sanity, I order my kids to the couch and play a movie. But most of the time, I prefer that they go outside to play, read a book, or find some other activity to occupy their time.

Over the years as my children have gotten older and more independent, they have each discovered activities they enjoy doing on their own. My oldest son plays bass guitar and has started a reptile breeding business. My middle son spends much of his time disassembling electronics and inventing new machines. My oldest daughter is a musician, while her younger sister loves to read and experiment in the kitchen. Even my youngest son, who is only six, will spend hours constructing elaborate Lego scenes. None are ever at a loss of how to spend their time.

As parents, not only are we responsible for the physical well-being of our children, we are also responsible for their mental and emotional well-being. Most parents would not knowingly feed their children poison or allow them to do something that would put their lives at risk, yet every day we plug our kids into something that study after study has shown to be detrimental to their cognitive health.

If you want your kids to reach their greatest potential, to develop their intellect and creativity to its fullest, then I invite you to turn off your TV and leave it off—for good.

SECRET # 5

MAKE WRITING FUN!

"I learned that you should feel when writing, not like Lord Byron on a mountain top, but like a child stringing beads in kindergarten - happy, absorbed and quietly putting one bead on after another." – Brenda Ueland

Any parent knows that if you want a kid to really hate something, just tell him he *has* to do it, or else.

In the classic children's film *Mary Poppins*, Jane and Michael Banks live in turn-of-the-century London. These conniving pranksters manage to chase away every nanny their father hires for them. Their parents are at the end of their ropes. Then Mary Poppins arrives. One of the first tasks she requests of the children is to pick up their room. Jane and Michael balk and whine. To them it is a tedious, pointless chore that they don't want to do. What does Mary Poppins do to change their attitude? She throws in a spoonful of sugar and makes the whole thing a game. In no time at all the room is clean and the children are tucked neatly in their beds.

Obviously, real life doesn't work quite like that. We have no magical carpetbag from which to pull out hat racks and measuring sticks. But we do have the same power Mary Poppins did to create a positive atmosphere of cooperation and optimism in our homes. The choice as to whether or not our children will hate what we ask them to do, or do it willingly and cheerfully, rests largely with us. As mentioned in the chapter *Secret #3: Throw Away the Red Pen*, like it or not, children generally take their attitude cues from their parents.

The Joy of Writing

This lesson about attitude was one I learned a little late in life and at a higher price than I would have cared to pay. I began homeschooling my son when he was eight years old. He had had some bad experiences in public school which left him with a low self-esteem and a raging temper. Overall, he was a sweet and loving child, until someone tried to force him to do something against his will. Then all hell would break loose.

I found myself not knowing how to handle his outbursts. I was at a loss as to whether I should punish him or embrace him. Teaching at home was especially difficult because he often refused to do the assignments. Unfortunately for both of us, I chose the wrong course of action. I tried to force him. I became inflexible in my demands. I stood over him like an armed guard to make sure he did every problem I asked of him. When he tried to get up from his chair, I held him down. *You will do it*! I demanded.

The result was not at all what I expected or wanted. The tantrums increased. Tears flowed. Voices were raised in sheer frustration. I was, in effect, making my son hate learning. Learning was for him something akin to breaking rocks is for a convict.

At about the same time I was struggling with my son, I also began teaching creative writing classes in my home. Of course, I would never dare raise my voice with other people's children. I was the ideal teacher, patient, encouraging, and enthusiastic. The results were magnificent. Children who came to me hating to write were transformed into eager writers filled with ideas they couldn't wait to get on paper.

Sadly, more than a year went by before it occurred to me that something was seriously wrong with this picture. My students were smiling and laughing in my classes while my own son was nearly in tears every day. I realized with near horror that I was the cause of my son's negative attitude. Because I placed demands on him that I would never have demanded of my students, he had come to hate school, and more specifically, writing.

Needless to say, I changed my approach. I released the reins, so to speak, and created a more relaxed atmosphere in our homeschool. After a while, he began to enjoy learning again. However, the damage done did not heal over night. It took a few years to undo all the damage done in school and at home. Today, thankfully, he is a successful high school student with plans to attend college next year.

Writing well demands that the writer enjoy writing. When writing becomes nothing more than an assignment with no purpose except to earn a grade on a report card, chances are good that the student will come to dread writing. It will become a chore just like washing the dishes or making his bed. True, there are those rare individuals who enjoy doing their chores well, but most kids prefer to do the minimum required to get the job done.

Is this the attitude you want your children to have toward writing? Do you want them to write a five-paragraph essay just to make you happy? Is that really the purpose of a writing education?

Of course not. The ultimate goal is for our children to feel confident in their writing skills, to enjoy writing, to see writing as a means of self-expression. But to achieve that goal requires that we, as adults, help our children find the joy in writing.

In my classes, I teach students how to write well. I do not, however, grade anything, nor do I spend much time critiquing their work. In fact, my students don't even realize they're learning to write well because they are so excited about what they are doing. Parent after parent has attested to the success of my course. Their children go on to write and write and write. These parents are often amazed at the transformation.

What is my secret?

I make writing fun.

To me, there is nothing more fun than sitting alone at my computer in the middle of the night to write. I would rather do that than just about anything else. The trick is how to transfer my own love of writing to my students. I do this by taking the focus off of writing. As far as my students are concerned, writing is a means to an end, a tool for getting what is inside their heads onto paper.

Think of words as if they were clay. The clay by itself is nothing but a gray lump on a potter's wheel. But in the hands of the potter, the clay begins to take shape. If the potter doesn't like the form, he can squash it and start all over again. He can do this over and over until he gets it just right. Once it is finished and the piece is fired and glazed, we see not the lump of clay, but a beautiful vase.

Writers use words to create something beautiful. We are not as concerned with the words themselves as we are with the finished product. When children focus on that finished product, be it a poem or play or story, words become tools, the medium by which they can bring their dreams to life.

Let's face it, not everyone wants to be a writer. Not everyone wants to be an architect, or a lawyer, or a physician either. Without desire, the motivation to succeed is low. You cannot expect every child to sit down at his desk and say, "I can't wait to write today!" However, since writing is a fundamental skill that everyone needs to function in our society, you must find some way to generate that desire within your child.

Intrinsic vs. Extrinsic Motivation

Extrinsic motivations (such as an allowance, extra time to play with friends, a day off of homework) work well when you want your children to complete a specific task like getting their bedroom clean or raking up the yard. However, the focus here is on the reward rather than the task.

With writing, the focus ought to be intrinsic to writing. The project itself, rather than hope of a reward, should become the motivation.

I taught a class on essay writing one year where I allowed the students to choose their own topics. One boy decided he wanted to write about dragons. His mother immediately intervened, telling him that dragons were not an appropriate topic for an essay. She steered him toward something she considered more realistic—komodo dragons. But Eddy* did not want to write about komodo dragons and quickly lost interest in the assignment.

I had a nice little chat with Mom and convinced her to let Eddy make his own decisions in regards to his essay. She backed off, and Eddy pursued his dragons. The topic eventually evolved from dragons to Yu-Gi-Oh, a popular trading card game. Again his mother went into panic mode, and again I assured her that Eddy would be just fine. His final essay was entitled "How To Play Yu-Gi-Oh" and was a detailed instructional piece for players new to the game. He put a lot of thought into the assignment, and he did it because it was a topic that he chose on his own and that interested him personally.

Schools often make the mistake of doling out writing assignments like they were a deck of cards. Kids get what they get whether they like it or not. If you want a child to enjoy writing, let him write about what interests him. That interest will inspire him and will become the motivation behind the writing. No other reward is necessary.

There are several methods I use to foster a love of writing in my students and in my own children. Which method I use depends on both the age and capability of the individual, as well as what is appropriate for each child's specific interests and needs. Remember, the ultimate objective is to help your child develop an "I can" attitude about writing. The first step toward that objective is to show your child just how fun writing can be.

POETRY

Poetry is a wonderful way to introduce children to writing. I begin with Haiku, a poem with three lines and a fixed number of syllables in each line. Then I move on to rhyme and meter. We learn the difference between doublets and quatrains and read several examples from various poets. Children of all ages, even teenagers, especially love funny poems. Once students learn the basic techniques of poetry, they are ready to write their own. Their first attempts are rarely perfect. There may be too many or two few syllables. Their imagery is simplistic. It doesn't matter. The grins on their faces as they read their poems to each other shows the pleasure and pride they reap from even the most modest of accomplishments.

JOURNAL/DIARY

If your child does not have a journal, get him one. Journal entries can vary from a single sentence to multiple pages. The student does not have to show what he writes to anyone else unless he chooses to. To start your child on the right track, set aside a few minutes of quiet time each day or once a week. If he seems disinterested or unsure of what to write, *suggest* a topic or two to get him started. Additionally, consider using this time to write in your journal as well. Children learn best by example.

FAMILY HISTORY

Writing a family history is a long-term project requiring research, organization and writing. Students may begin by interviewing a selected member of the family, such as a grandparent, to find out about his/her life. Interviews can be recorded on cassette and later transcribed. Students can compile written stories with photographs and other memorabilia in a book. Such books can then be replicated and shared with other members of the family.

PERSONAL LETTERS

Letters to friends and loved ones are a painless way to get your children to write. When your child receives a gift for his birthday from a distant relative, encourage him to write a thank you note. If you plan to send a letter with your Christmas cards, have your child write the letter for you. Pen pals, missionaries, and soldiers all enjoy receiving letters and can give your child the opportunity to practice his writing skills.

BOOK REPORTS

I am not very fond of assigned book reports per se. However, I am a huge fan of creativity and ingenuity. When I taught American Literature one year, I divided the class into small groups. Each group was given a choice of projects, which they presented to the rest of the class. The choices included designing a book cover with a summary, author bio, and blurbs; writing a dramatized scene from the book and performing it; creating a travel advertisement for the book's setting; and to either write a sequel to the book or rewrite the ending. I was always amazed at how much effort went into these projects and how much fun the students had doing them.

ESSAYS

As much as we all groan at the thought of having to write an essay, learning how to organize, research and compile information and then compose an essay is vital for anyone planning to apply to college. However, essays do not need to be boring or hard. I recommend letting your child choose a topic that is of great interest to him, something that he wants to know more about. Teach him the techniques of brainstorming, outlining, drafting and revising one step at a time. The work of writing will soon fade into the background as he learns about his favorite subject.

ILLUSTRATED STORIES

This is a great choice for students who have an artistic flair. Most of us are familiar with comic books, illustrated action-based stories with scenes laid out in individual boxes on the page. Manga (which originated in Japan) are very similar to traditional comics, but are not limited to superhero plots. Some manga can be quite complex. Students who enjoy sketching or painting can create a sequence of images, and then add dialogue and narration to help carry the story along. Children's picture books are another form of narrating images, but the stories are usually more simplistic and pictures are one to a page.

FICTION

This is my method of choice. In my opinion, there is no better way to help kids fall in love with writing than by teaching them how to write stories. Even children as young as four and five years old can learn to write stories. I start them off with story*telling*. We sit in a circle and I introduce a character and the beginning of a story. Then each person takes a turn and adds something to the story. This simple exercise exposes children to the concepts that they will later develop in their writing. Once they are capable of writing even simple sentences and paragraphs, children can learn to write a story. And of course, the older the child is, the more complex the stories become. It has been my experience that once a child writes one story, they will go on to write many, many more.

SCRIPTS FOR STAGE & SCREEN

This is a different form of writing than most of the other methods previously mentioned. For one thing, approximately 95% of what is written in a play is dialogue. The other 5% is divided between brief descriptions of characters and settings, and action. Some kids love to write plays and perform them. I wrote many plays when I was growing up. The most important thing a parent can do to support their child playwright is to be a captive audience. When your daughter tells you to sit down and watch her play, sit down and watch it. Then applaud, applaud, applaud.

SONG LYRICS

Writing lyrics is a lot like writing poetry. The difference is that you set the words to music. A fun way to introduce this form of writing to your child is to make up new words to songs he already knows. For young children, make up new words to "Old Mac Donald," or "The Wheels on the Bus." Older children and teens are especially good at this. Take a popular tune from the radio and add new words and phrases. Encourage them to write their songs in their journals.

FLYERS/INVITATIONS/GROCERY LISTS/ETC.

Basically, this is a *catch all* category. Your child can probably write anything that needs to be written in your home. Ask your child to add items to your grocery list. Make a list of chores and have your child create a chart for them. Have your teens design flyers for your garage sale or invitations to her birthday party on the computer. The possibilities are truly endless.

Carsten's Story

The first time Carsten walked into my dining room, he was ten years old and not too happy to be there. One of twelve homeschool students who had enrolled in my first ever creative writing class, Carsten made it very clear that he would rather be home playing video games than write anything at all. Carsten was a nice boy, polite and well-behaved, but his attention span was about as long as his little finger. Within a few minutes he began fidgeting in his chair. Soon after that, he asked how many minutes were left in the class, a question he repeated a dozen times over the course of the hour. Shortly before I actually ended the class, Carsten stood up and walked out of the house. He had had enough for the day.

To my surprise, Carsten kept coming to class. Each week was a repeat of the week before. I was convinced that his mother was forcing him to come, perhaps hoping for a miracle of some sort. I believed that this may be the one child I would be unable to help.

At the end of the session, Carsten brought his finished story to class. It was an action adventure story, like Indiana Jones, and it was really, really rough around the edges. Still, I was pleased that he had at least completed the assignment. I never expected to see Carsten again.

Yet Carsten kept coming. He ended up attending three creative writing sessions over the course of two years. His stories, which were mostly fan fiction based on Star Wars, grew by both length and complexity. At one point, his mother expressed concern that writing by hand was a struggle for him. I suggested that he dictate his stories to her while she typed them on the computer. She agreed.

Not long after that she told me what had happened. It seemed that Carsten loved creating stories and would dictate them to his mother on a regular basis. Then one day he grew impatient with her slow typing and told her to let him try. She got up from the computer and watched as he began to type his own story.

One night his father spied him typing late into the night. Thinking he was playing video games, he told Carsten that it was time to go to bed.

"I'm writing my story," replied Carsten.

His father quietly closed the door, happy his son finally was enjoying writing. As time went on, Carsten's typing improved. Soon he had written a dozen different stories and had plans to write more.

When his younger brother enrolled in my creative writing class for the first time, Carsten offered to help him write his story. Today Carsten is now learning to write essays. He is writing his first essay about a space probe he plans to build one day and send to Jupiter. And he's writing his rough draft by hand.

Carsten is a prime example of how a reluctant writer can be transformed into an enthusiastic writer with a little bit of flexibility and freedom. Now every time I see him he has a new story to share with me. Carsten taught me that every child can learn to write well and deserves the opportunity to discover how wonderful writing can be!

SECRET #6

RAISE THE BAR

"Only those who risk going too far can possibly find out how far they can go." – T.S. Eliot

Have you ever watched a high jump competition? In the high jump, competitors must run and jump, clearing a bar suspended between two erect poles. At the beginning of the competition, the bar is set relatively low. As the competitor clears his jumps, the bar is raised in measured increments. With each successive attempt, the competitor pushes himself a little bit more.

It is interesting to note that in 1895 the men's high jump world record was set at just under 6 ½ feet. Since then, record heights have steadily increased. Today the record stands at 8 ½ feet, a vivid testimony to the seemingly limitless boundaries of the human body and spirit.

We hear story upon story of individuals who triumph over impossible obstacles. While we admire them for their accomplishments, we also tell ourselves we could never do that. The truth is we could do *that*, whatever *that* might be—if we really wanted to.

My mother has a saying that is a great motivation in her life: "If someone else has done it, I can learn to do it, too." Admittedly, some things take a lot more effort than others, but my mother's saying is true. How did Sally Ride become an astronaut? How did George W. Bush become the President of the United States? How did Bill Gates become the owner of a multi-billion dollar corporation? The answer is: they wanted it, and they worked for it. The same holds true for every goal we set in life, no matter how big or small it may be.

One Step at a Time

Not long ago I decided to go on a weight loss plan. In addition to changing my eating habits, I also needed to exercise. The problem was that I hated to exercise. I groaned at the idea of lifting weights, doing aerobics, or even walking.

I decided to start with something small, a short stroll down the block two or three times a week. A friend of mine invited me to join her on her morning walks, and though I accepted her invitation, it was not without some serious reservations. Would I be capable of walking what amounted to an entire mile? If I did succeed, would I be willing to do it a second time?

The first day my friend and I walked for thirty minutes. Our pace was brisk, and I felt winded the entire way. I struggled to make the last few yards home. I was hot and sweaty. My muscles ached. My legs wobbled as I dragged myself up the short flight of stairs to my front door.

Could I do this three times a week? Would I survive even long enough to make it to my shower?

Despite my doubts and still aching legs, I met my friend two days later for another walk. To my surprise, my legs felt a little stronger this time, and I seemed to recover more quickly.

I kept on walking with my friend. Each time we went, my body felt a little bit stronger. After several weeks, our walk had become almost too easy for me.

I decided it was time to kick things up a notch.

One morning, I left my house and started walking down the street toward the spot where my friend and I usually met. I wanted to get there before she did that day, so I ran—or rather jogged—one block. I thought I would keel over and die on the spot. My lungs burned from the chill morning air. My leg muscles cramped up. I bent over and grabbed my knees, gasping for breath. It was the hardest thirty seconds I had experienced in a long, long time. But I had done it. I reached our spot before my friend.

The next time we were to walk, I decided to jog a little farther. I wondered if I would be able to make it half way to her home. I picked up speed, and almost immediately the burning in my chest flared up, but I kept going. I didn't make it as far as I had planned, but it was farther than the time before.

Finally, I wanted to jog all the way to my friend's house, about a third of a mile from my home. I had never jogged that far in my entire life. I worried that I might go into cardiac arrest before reaching my goal, or that I might faint from oxygen deprivation. As my feet began to hit the pavement in a rhythmic pattern, I glanced up and realized, to my dismay, that the street curved to the left so that my friend's house was blocked from view.

I had thought that if I kept my eyes on my goal, it would be easier to get there. But it was nowhere in sight. I started to feel discouraged. Maybe I should just stop, I told myself. Her house is too far anyway. I've never gone that far before. How could I possibly do it now?

But instead of stopping I changed my focus. I spotted a thin-trunked tree a few yards ahead of me. I'll just jog to that tree, I said.

As I reached the tree I decided that I wasn't that tired yet, so instead of stopping, I again shifted my focus to a streetlight another few yards ahead. I did the same when I reached that goal and ran to an RV, then a fire hydrant, and another tree. Finally the street straightened and I could see my friend's house not far in the distance. I kept my eyes on the house and jogged all the way to the front step.

I learned several important things from that experience. The first thing I learned is that sometimes our goals, as noble and important though they are, are too far away. When our goals are too large, too far in the distance, they may seem almost impossible to reach. We can become discouraged and convince ourselves that we cannot achieve them. So we give up.

In 1974, seventeen-year-old long distance swimmer Lynne Cox attempted to swim the twenty-seven miles from Catalina Island to the California mainland. When a heavy fog cut visibility to nearly zero, Lynne panicked. She was separated from her escort boats and felt something brush against her in the dark water. When the boat reappeared, Lynne grabbed an oar and was pulled to safety, ending her swim.

Because she lost sight of her destination and let fear obscure her goal, she gave up. If that were the end of her story, one might conclude that setting goals too far out of reach leads only to failure. However, Lynne Cox's story does not end there. Not by a long shot.

The other lesson I learned from my own experiences is that any worthy goal is possible to achieve when the right course of action is taken. The only way we can fail is when we choose to fail. But no objective is achieved without a plan or effort. It is best to take that objective and break it down into smaller, more immediate goals. Instead of trying to head for my friend's house that seemed so impossibly far, I aimed for closer targets and reached them one at a time until I finally arrived at my desired destination.

After Lynne Cox's failed Catalina swim, she went back and succeeded not only in swimming the distance between the mainland and the island, but she set a world record doing it. She then went on to set records swimming the Bering Strait, the Cook Strait, the Strait of Magellan, and many, many others. Today she is a world-renowned swimmer and author because for her, failure was never an option.

Know Your Goal

The lessons mentioned above can be applied to any goal, whether it is to graduate from college, learn a musical instrument, plan for financial retirement, or become proficient in writing. To make the journey easier to travel, large or long-term goals are best achieved when broken down into smaller more attainable objectives.

In the case of teaching your child to write well, the first thing you should do is *know your goal*. What do you expect to be the final destination of your child's writing education? Do you want him to be able to get into a good university? To write better than you do? To go into a writing career?

Your goal will depend heavily on your child's expectations of himself. If your child wants to be a writer when he grows up, then your goal should be to help him achieve that. If your child is struggling with the fundamentals, your goal might be to bring his skills up to grade level. Maybe your teenager is preparing for the SAT or a college entrance examination and he needs to hone his writing skills in order to improve his chances of being accepted. Whatever your desired destination may be, set your goal accordingly.

Another factor to consider is your child's abilities. If he has a learning disability or handicap that makes reading and writing difficult, that will affect your goal. If your child is a teenager whose foundation in writing is weak, you may need to alter your expectations a little. Goals should not be unrealistic or unattainable. They should be well enough within reach so that your child does not become easily discouraged or frustrated. A little struggle is good, but if there is no end to the struggle, your child will simply give up.

David's Story

David* was nine years old when he enrolled in my homeschool speech and debate class. He was energetic and well-mannered, a delight to have in my class. The first day of class I asked my students to take turns reading from our workbook. Several students took their turns. Then I called on David.

I waited for several moments, but he did not respond. Thinking he had not heard me, I called his name again. He sat quietly, staring at the page in front of him. It occurred to me that maybe he was shy. If so, he was certainly not the first shy student I had had, so instead of putting him on the spot, I simply called the next person's name, and the reading continued.

The following week the same thing occurred. This time, however, David tried to read. He struggled with even the simplest words and gave up halfway through the first sentence. I assumed that he couldn't read yet. I praised him for his efforts and again moved on to the next student.

When I mentioned the experience to his mother, I expressed concern because much of the coming weeks would require reading out loud. Students were to learn a famous historical speech and perform it in front of our entire homeschool group. If David could not read, how would he be able to learn his speech?

As it turned out, my assumption was incorrect. David could read just fine. The problem was his eyes. His eyesight was very weak. He could hardly make out the words on a page. His mother wanted to pull David out of the class. She thought it might be too much of a struggle for him. However, I asked that she give him a chance and suggested that she help him read the assignments at home so that when he came to class, he would already be familiar with them. She agreed.

The next week, students were to bring a storybook from home and read out loud from it to the class. David brought Shel Silverstein's *The Giving Tree*. When his turn came, he breezed through the first half of the book with almost no mistakes. I was so impressed that I asked him to continue. He tried to read the next few words but could not.

"I didn't learn this part," he told me.

It was then I realized that he had memorized the entire first half of the book.

David kept coming to class. His hesitations soon disappeared and he became enthusiastic and excited about his assignments. His mother bought him a hand-held magnifying glass to help him see print better. When other students struggled to sound out words, David generously offered his glass to them.

His reading was often slow and labored, but everyone patiently waited as he read. He smiled proudly at every accomplishment. Finally, after many weeks of preparation, performance day arrived. As the audience gathered on the park bleachers, I looked for David. There he was, grasping his speech firmly in his hand. A wide smile adorned his face. When it was his turn to give his presentation, he stood tall and straight, the shyness that nearly crippled him weeks earlier was completely gone. When he was finished, the audience applauded, unaware of just how great a victory he had actually won.

Learning from Mistakes

We humans do not like struggle. When possible, we usually seek the path of least resistance. But it is the resistance that makes us strong. The principle of resistance is what adds mass to muscle, holds up bridges, and creates energy and heat. Without resistance, humankind would never have devised so many marvelous inventions to overcome it. If David had quit my class, he may never have discovered a way to overcome his disability. So, why do so many parents inadvertently try to shelter their children from struggle?

It is perfectly normal for a mother to want to comfort her child when he falls and skins his knee, but should she never let him ride a bicycle for fear that he will one day fall? Should she keep him from making friends with other children because one of those friends might hurt his feelings? Of course not.

Parents know that struggle and resistance play a vital role in growing up. Yet when it comes to learning how to write well, many parents fail to urge their children onward. Either they think it is not important enough, or they wish to protect their children from having the same bad experiences they had as a child. Certainly, some bad experiences should never repeat themselves, but others are perfectly acceptable.

Returning again to my own experiences in school, I would never wish a Ms. Danson on any child. However, there is nothing wrong with making mistakes and learning from them. And that, perhaps, is the key to making resistance pay off: learning from our mistakes.

When your child writes his first short story, for example, he will undoubtedly make many mistakes, but perfection is not the goal. The goal is for your child to become a better writer.

To accomplish that goal, you must set smaller goals. Perhaps his first goal could be to find his own punctuation and/or spelling mistakes and correct them. Another goal would be to rewrite the story and include dialogue. Yet another goal would be to correct improper grammar, and so forth. Each successive goal builds on the one previous, like embarking on a journey by taking one step at a time.

A child who is too focused on perfection will see his mistakes as flaws in himself. He will become discouraged and might respond by tearing up his story or throwing his pencil down in frustration. This is not what we want to happen. If your child has this kind of response to writing, it is a good bet that either you or he has spent too much time worrying about being perfect. Do not criticize or nag your child into writing. Such strategies will only backfire. Instead, gently urge your child to pace his writing according to his comfort level. Teach him that mistakes are okay. Everyone makes them. They can be easily corrected. As I mentioned earlier, learning to write well is a process rather than a destination.

Once a child realizes that no one is going to slap a grade on his writing, and that he will not be criticized or condemned for his mistakes, he will begin to write more often and with more enthusiasm.

The Path of Least Resistance

Just as resistance without progress leads to failure, too little resistance will do the same. Imagine for a moment that your ten-year-old writes an essay about his favorite animal. Immediately you notice several glaring problems. First, the essay is barely a paragraph long. Second, nearly every word is misspelled. Punctuation and grammar errors are everywhere. What would happen if you were to read the essay, praise your child without offering any suggestions for improvement, and give it back?

Your child's ego would certainly receive a good boost, but he would have a distorted view of his accomplishments. He would not learn to recognize his mistakes nor how to correct them. If similar experiences continue, the quality of his writing will likely never improve. He will get older, but he will continue writing as though he was in third or fourth grade. When it comes time for him to apply for college or a job, he may be stunned to discover that he lacks the skills necessary to obtain the goals he desires.

No parent wants her child to fail in this way. So it is important that you allow him to experience a healthy amount of resistance in life. Each time your child achieves a small objective, you must raise the bar of expectation a little bit more. Of course, you will be there right beside him to help him along the way. When he stumbles and falls, as he is bound to do from time to time, he may want to give up. Don't let him. Just help him back on his feet and keep urging him forward.

A man named C. Hunter Boyd once said, "Last is just the slowest winner." It does not matter if your child is the best writer in his class or that he skips ahead a grade because he is a whiz with grammar. What matters is that he learns what he needs to learn to get ahead in the world. Raise your expectations of your child. and he will raise his expectations of himself. If he takes just one step at a time, someday he will glance over his shoulder and discover he has traveled miles.

I happened on a poem not long ago that I think perfectly illustrates this concept. It is called "The Quitter," and was written by Gene Thibeault:

When you're lost on the trail with the speed of a snail
And defeat looks you straight in the eye
And you're needing to sit, your whole being says quit
You're certain it's your time to die.
But the code of the trail is "move forward don't fail"
Though your knees and ego are scarred.
All the swelling and pain is just part of the game
In the long run it's quitting that's hard!

"I'm sick of the pain!" Well, now, that's a shame
But you're strong, you're healthy, and bright.
So you've had a bad stretch and you're ready to retch,
Shoulders back, move forward, and fight.
It's the plugging away that will win you the day,
Now don't be a loser my friend!
So the goal isn't near, why advance to the rear.
All struggles eventually end.

It's simple to cry that you're finished; and die.
It's easy to whimper and whine.
Move forward and fight, though there's no help in sight
You'll soon cross the lost finish line.
You'll come out of the black, with the wind at your back,
As the clouds start to part; there's the sun.
Then you'll know in your heart, as you did at the start.
You're not a quitter. You've Won!!

PART 2: THE MECHANICS OF LEARNING

THE 7 STAGES OF A WRITING EDUCATION

In the past two decades, research in neuroscience has come to better understand the process by which the human brain develops and learns. From the time we are born, we have a tremendous capacity to learn, but the rate and efficiency at which we learn depends heavily on the experiences that can only be provided by the adults in our lives. In other words, the more stimulation a parent or caretaker creates for his/her child, the more that child will learn. This learning occurs as a child senses the world around him, allowing billions of neural connections to form within the brain.

According to early 20th century psychologist Jean Piaget, children progress through four cognitive developmental stages. From birth to age

2, children experience the Sensorimotor stage, in which they acquire knowledge through physically manipulating and interacting with their environment. From ages 2 to 7, children progress through the Preoperational stage during, where they develop language and participate in pretend play. In the Concrete Operational stage, from ages 7 to 11, children begin to think more logically but still struggle with abstract or hypothetical ideas. Finally, in the Formal Operational stage, adolescents develop the ability to understand abstract ideas and use deductive reasoning.

Piaget formulated these stages while observing his own children. However, having a Ph.D. is not necessary to understand how learning takes place. Like Piaget, many parents come to grasp how their children learn by making similar observations in their own homes.

Combining my own observations with Piaget's stages, I came up with a slightly modified version of developmental stages to help parents know how best to interact with their children at certain times. This chapter breaks down the process of learning to write according to a child's age. However, these are simply general guidelines. Some children develop and mature faster than others. Some develop a little slower. For this reason, I have given a rather wide age range for each category, and some categories overlap. For example, even though I suggest that an eight-year-old should be writing paragraphs, if your eight-year-old is still struggling with simple sentences, don't panic!

Not long ago, a mother expressed concern that her nine-year-old son showed no interest in writing. He didn't even like reading all that much. She wondered if there was something wrong with him. After asking several questions to determine if he was developing normally in other aspects, I told the mother not to worry. It is normal for some boys to prefer climbing trees and riding skateboards to cuddling up with a book or writing his life history.

This is not to say that learning disabilities do not exist. They do exist and often pose a serious threat to a child's development and education. If you suspect that your child has a learning disability, have him evaluated by a trained specialist immediately. You can obtain a referral to a specialist in your area through your family physician or your local school district office.

In the meantime, use the following guide as just that, a guide. Accompanying each stage is a brief description of where a child should be in the process of learning to write and what parents can do to help them along. Bulleted lists are included as a quick reference.

FORMATIVE STAGE
(6 months to 3 years)

The most important thing you can do during your child's formative years to prepare him to write well is to read to him. Make reading together a special part of your daily schedule. Studies have shown that children develop reading, listening, speaking and writing skills simultaneously.[20] Reading out loud to your children is perhaps the most effective way of encouraging this development.

- *Read out loud to your child every day*

PREPATORY STAGE
(3 to 5 years)

Preschool-aged children love to mimic their parents' behavior. By this time, they have pretty

---

[20] Nagin, 33

well mastered the English language and are able to articulate their most tangible thoughts and desires. Introduce writing now. Teach them the letters of the alphabet and the sounds they make. Encourage children to trace letters and numbers, first with their fingers, and then with a crayon or a pencil. Children at this stage want to know how to spell their names, and many will learn how to write their names. Holding your child's hand in yours as you write her name together is fun and effective. Repetition and patience are vital in this stage. Praise any effort on their part.

- *Letters of the alphabet*
- *Sounds of the letters*
- *Trace letters*
- *Spell & write child's name*
- *Repetition, patience, and praise*

EXPLORATORY STAGE
(5 to 8 years)

Questions, questions, and more questions! It can drive even the most tolerant parent to insanity. This is the time when your child is gathering and processing information about his environment. He is discovering the symbolic nature of both spoken and written language. Younger children ask how to spell everything. While this is understandably annoying to you as an adult, it is important that you go ahead and spell for him. Answer his questions. Lead him to books that can answer his questions and read them together. During this time it is imperative that your child's natural curiosity and enthusiasm NOT be stifled by criticism, impatience, or unrealistic expectations.

Some children will begin reading books on their own. As your child develops his reading skills, encourage him to write as well. Purchase a journal where your child can jot down words or ideas that interest him. Teach the difference between capital and lowercase letters. Older children should learn to write simple sentences and to capitalize the first letter in a sentence and end it with a period. This is also the time to start a portfolio of your child's writing.

- *Answer questions*
- *Spell words out loud*
- *Purchase a journal*
- *Encourage writing words and simple sentences*

- *Teach capital and lowercase letters and their proper use*
- *Explain that periods go at the end of a sentence*
- Start a portfolio

EXPERIMENTATION STAGE
(6 to 9 years)

Most children this age are capable of learning the basic parts of speech and punctuation. Help them connect spoken language with written language. Introduce storytelling games and teach them how to write poetry. Have them draw pictures and add their own text on the bottom. Put these pictures in a book and have your child read it to his younger siblings.

Writing at this stage should be an adventure, like learning how the pieces of a puzzle fit together to form a picture. Parts of speech and punctuation are the pieces of the puzzle, while complete thoughts, ideas, and even stories are the picture. Children on the older end of this age range should be taught to write paragraphs. Suggest various topics of interest and have them write for several minutes about it. A good rule of thumb is for the child to write the same number of sentences as his age. On a regular basis, ask your child to choose the best writing sample from his portfolio to read out loud to the rest of the family.

- *Teach basic parts of speech & punctuation*
- *Introduce storytelling*
- *Read and write poetry*
- *Add narration to pictures and make a book*
- *Write complete paragraphs*
- *Students select examples from portfolio to share with family*

PROGRESSIVE STAGE
(9 to 12 years)

Older children speak in increasingly complex sentences and can easily correlate what they say to what they write. Teach them how to use a dictionary in order to check the spelling and meaning of words that are new to them. Encourage good penmanship. Introduce fiction writing. Teach them about characterization, plot, setting, imagery, etc.

Keep your focus on the process of creating the story rather than on the writing. Stories should be written in at least two or three drafts. Your child should read his drafts out loud to spot mistakes and correct them. He should then revise them.

In addition to fiction, children may also create projects or write reports about their favorite books and write two or three paragraph essays about topics of interest. Positive adult feedback is essential at this stage. Help students recognize their mistakes and make suggestions for improvement. Reinforce writing rules. Make sure your child knows how to format paragraphs correctly, including margins, line spacing, and indenting. Consider enrolling your child in a writing class or writers' group. Also, purchase a typing program or enroll him in a typing class.

- *Complex sentences, tenses, and possessives*
- *Utilize five senses in writing*
- *Short stories, poetry, simple essays*
- *Write rough draft, edit draft for mistakes, write final draft*
- *Begin typing instruction*
- *Positive adult feedback*
- *Penmanship*
- *Formatting a paragraph*
- *Join a writing class or writers' group*

INDEPENDENT STAGE
(12 to 14 years)

At this stage, students should be writing regularly in a journal, as well as writing poetry, stories, letters, etc. on their own. Adult feedback should continue to be positive but should evolve to include constructive criticism in order to help students to progress. Students should be able to brainstorm ideas for essays, conduct research, and create an outline. Essays should include accurate facts, quotations from published sources, and a bibliography. Teach them how to write an effective introduction and conclusion. Several drafts should be written for each project. Fiction should be compelling. Dialogue and imagery should be present. Plot and characters should be well-developed.

- *Brainstorming & outlining*
- *Research skills*
- *Five paragraph essay (informative)*
- *Fiction should be engaging and include dialogue and imagery*
- *Parents should offer constructive criticism*

MASTERY STAGE
(14 years & up)

Students at this age should be preparing for the SAT and looking ahead toward college admission. Essays and stories should have attention-grabbing openings and clearly defined conclusions. Vocabulary should be diverse. Spelling errors should be few. Students should have a good grasp of grammar and be able to use punctuation, including commas and quotation marks, correctly. Additionally, students should be able to articulate complex ideas, as well as present and support a persuasive argument.

Later in this stage, parents should offer passive support. Students will ask for assistance when needed. However, if you notice a glaring weakness that keeps repeating itself, point it out to your child and make suggestions on how to correct the problem. Writing on a daily basis will help develop skills further. Encourage students to share their writing with other adults, such as a mentor or tutor, who can provide constructive criticism.

- *Prepare for SAT & college admission*
- *Diverse vocabulary*
- *Few spelling and grammar errors*

- *Correct use of punctuation*
- *Persuasive essay*
- *Daily writing to improve skills*
- *Adults provide passive support*
- *Suggest ways to improve*
- *Share writing with other adults who will provide constructive criticism*

WRITING STRATEGIES THAT WORK

B y following the six secrets described in this book, you will help to create a positive learning environment in your home, which will translate to a positive attitude toward writing in your child. However, to ensure that your child's writing education is successful, several additional elements are needed. The more of these elements that you utilize, the more progress will occur.

You may notice that drills and worksheets are not included on this list. Such techniques have not been found to improve writing skills. What does improve writing is the process of writing itself, including planning, research, drafting and revising, all of which are incorporated into the techniques below.

While this list is by no means exhaustive, it represents those techniques that are most effective and which are used in successful writing programs nationwide.

Pre-writing

This is the planning stage of writing, where the student decides what topic to write about in an essay or how the plot of his story will progress. Brainstorming, research, and creating an outline become the skeletal framework on which his words will hang. I tell my students that writing is like traveling in the car and the outline is like a map. You ought to know where you are going before you even turn on the engine. While the descriptions below relate to writing essays, the techniques can be equally applied to all forms of writing.

> ***Brainstorming:*** This is a way to get all the jumbled ideas in one's head onto paper where it can be sorted into viable choices and possibilities. There are several different methods that can be used. The first is used to

narrow broad topics down to one that can be managed in a short essay. This is done by writing down a general topic at the top of the page, such as ANIMALS. Below that, write a more specific topic: MARSUPIALS. Below that, an even more specific topic: KANGAROOS. And finally, a very narrow topic, which will become the subject of the essay: WHY KANGAROOS HAVE POCKETS.

Another brainstorming method involves taking a broad topic, such as the one listed above, and writing down everything you can possibly think of connected to that topic. Items can be written as a long list or all over the page. Once everything is down, circle those items that are most interesting and use those as the basis for the essay.

Still another method is called *webbing* and is especially useful in determining supporting details and sub-topics. The main topic is written in the middle of the page and circled. Possible sub-topics are written all around it and are connected to it by drawing a line. Additional details may be added and connected to the sub-topics in the same manner.

Research: It is imperative that students learn how to conduct effective research. Research is not only necessary for writing essays, but it is also very useful in writing family histories and fiction. A vast amount of research can be done online via the internet. However, students should utilize their public libraries as well. Books, periodicals, encyclopedias, and videos are all useful tools.

As students conduct research, they should keep detailed notes that can later be used in their writing. Quotes should be written down verbatim, and the title and page number of the source cited. Any sources used for research should be cited in a bibliography, and quotes or references used in the writing should be footnoted.

A fun way to conduct research that also improves verbal communication skills is interviewing experts. I require my essay students to interview one expert and to include facts from the interview along with data gathered from other sources. The students choose someone who knows more about the subject than the average person (preferably someone who has personal experience with it), then call to make an appointment. Interviews can be conducted in person or on the phone. Students should make a list of questions prior to the actual interview and take notes during their conversation. If the interview is recorded, the student should first ask permission to do so. A thank you note should be sent immediately following the interview, and a copy of the final draft should also be sent.

Outlining: Once the topic and sub-topics have been chosen, and information has been gathered, write an outline. State the topic and then write the introduction to the essay. The introduction serves to explain to the audience what the essay is about and to catch the audience's attention.

Following the introduction, list each of the main sub-topics, or supporting topics. In a five-paragraph essay there are three supporting topics. Beneath each sub-topic are the supporting details, which may include statistics, interesting facts, quotations, etc.

The last thing to write in the outline is the conclusion, which is a summary of what your essay was about and how you feel about it.

Editing & Revising

Writing is a process. Few writers, if any, ever write a perfect piece on the first try. Even the most experienced and talented writers write many drafts, each one improving the end product a little bit more. Whether your child writes essays, poetry, short stories, or plays, he should understand that writing is always in a constant state of flux. I tell my students that nothing they write is permanent. Until their book is published and sitting on a shelf at Barnes & Noble, they can always make corrections and changes any time they like. When planning a writing project, expect to write multiple drafts.

The *first* or *rough draft* is when the student just *writes*. Do not be overly concerned with getting everything just right. Mistakes will be most prevalent here, and that's okay. The main purpose of the first draft is to get thoughts and ideas out of the head onto paper. When writing the first drafts of my novels, I never look back. I do not reread anything. I do not correct anything. My objective is to get to the end, to finish what I start. With this as the goal, all pressure for perfection is removed, and delays and writer's block are kept to a minimum.

The *working draft* is where ideas are refined, words and even entire paragraphs are rearranged, added, or deleted. Read the draft out loud. Look for the overall flow of the piece. Do you say what you want to say? Are your points expressed clearly and in an orderly manner?

Read the working draft again. Spelling, punctuation, and grammar errors are best spotted once all the words and ideas are in the right place. Check your format. Are the paragraphs indented? Do your quotes have quotation marks? You may also use this opportunity to improve vocabulary. Use a thesaurus to replace dull, uninteresting words with words that are more specific and appealing. There may be several working drafts between the first and final drafts.

The *final draft* is what you get when you are finished making all your revisions. This is as close to perfection as you're going to get, but it is not finished yet. Now other people can read it. Of course, when they do, they might spot some problems you didn't notice before. You can, of course, write as many or as few drafts as you like until you are satisfied with the finished product.

Portfolios

Artists keep samples of their artwork in portfolios. Authors do the same. Students may keep samples (or clips) of their writing in a binder or file box. Keep early drafts as well as final drafts. As time passes, it is interesting to go back and see how far you have progressed.

It is recommended that students occasionally select what they consider to be their best work to share with the family. After reading it out loud, he may wish to display it where others can read it. After a week or two, select a new piece and display that while filing the older one away.

It is recommended that portfolios contain physical copies of your writing as computer files can be corrupted and lost. However, do make back-ups of all your work on diskette and keep it in your portfolio as well.

Peer Evaluation

One of the most effective ways to generate enthusiasm for writing is for students to work in a group of their peers. Enrolling your child in a writing class or including him in a writers' group allows him to make friends with other kids who are learning and experiencing the same things he is. He will see that he is not the only one with questions or concerns about his writing. He will hear others' ideas and contribute to group discussions.

In my classes, I encourage students to give feedback to each other. When one student shares a sample of her writing with the class, the other students first give at least one specific compliment. Perhaps they like her use of metaphors, or a certain line of dialogue is especially interesting. Then they suggest one or two improvements. The opening needs to hook the reader. The main character needs more description. I encourage students to write their suggestions on paper as well as share them verbally.

In addition, I often divide the class into smaller groups of two or three students. One student reads to the others and then receives feedback. Then the roles are reversed. This smaller group allows for open discussion and helps students to build a rapport with one another. When students come to trust each another, their confidence grows.

If no writing class is available, consider starting a writers' group. Groups may meet at the library or a local bookstore. Sometimes these facilities may already host a writers' group. Check to see if the group is appropriate for children or teens. If not, start your own.

Publishing

Nothing is more exciting to a young writer than seeing his name in print. Publishing does not necessarily mean selling your work to a national publisher. Rather, it means taking your very best work and putting it in a permanent, attractive format. If you have written a poem, write it on parchment in calligraphy and have it framed. A short story or essay can be printed on quality paper with a unique font and given to someone special as a gift. Longer works, such as a novel or collection of stories or essays, can even be self-published with an online publisher such as Create Space, Kindle Direct Publishing, Smashwords, or Lulu.

Following each session of my creative writing classes, I have my students email their stories to me. After some editing on my part, I compile the stories into an 80-90 page book and publish it through Lulu. The end result is a high quality paper back with a color cover (designed by my students.) Students purchase them at cost to either keep or to give away to grandparents and other relatives. The kids love it, and once they experience being published, they are forever "bitten by the writing bug."

Of course, even children can be published in local newspapers and magazines. NewPages.com provides listings of publications and contests that accept submissions by children and teenagers. Also, *Writers Market* (by Writers Digest Books), which lists publishers alphabetically, signifies those publishers accepting material by minors with a picture of an apple.

I encourage my older students who show promise as writers to submit to contests and publishers. More often than not, they will be rejected. Most authors are. However, the experience will serve to motivate them to continue improving their skills as writers and to realize that reaching for the stars is not an impossible dream. They will have learned that if they only keep reaching, one day that dream, whatever it may be, will be within their grasp.

CONCLUSION

Learning to write well opens unimaginable doors for children, opportunities to excel in school, obtain employment, express themselves articulately, and follow their dreams. The lack of effective writing skills can actually be a handicap into today's world where such skills are so necessary for success in so many areas.

Included in this book are suggestions for creating a writing-friendly environment in your home and techniques for teaching writing and making writing fun for your child. There are also explanations about the process of learning to write and the different developmental steps involved in that process.

I hope that by reading *Teaching Your Kids to Write Well: Six Secrets Every Grown-Up Should Know*, you will feel more confident in your role as your child's teacher, and that, along with your child, you will discover the joy of writing.

ABOUT THE AUTHOR

After spending more than a decade as a newspaper editorialist, magazine staff writer, and book editor, Laurisa, a veteran homeschool mom, finally started living her dream of being an author. She is the author of four novels, the editor-in-chief of *Middle Shelf Magazine*, and senior editor of Skyrocket Press. She holds a Master's degree in English and lives in Southern California with her husband and five children.

Website: www.laurisawhitereyes.com
Blog: laurisareyes.blogspot.com

WORKS CITED

Cherry, Kendra. "Piaget's Stages of Cognitive Development." *Psychology.about.com*. About Education, n.d. Web. 11 March 2015.

"Declining SAT Scores: What Happened?" *educationwonk.blogspot.com*. The Education Wonks, 30 August 2006. Web. 24 Sep 2014.

Friel, John C., Ph. D & Friel, Linda D., M.A. *The 7 Worst Things Good Parents Do*. Deerfield Beach, FL: Health Communications, Inc., 1999. Print.

Gatto, John Taylor. *Dumbing Us Down: The Hidden Curriculum of Compulsory School*. Gabriola Island, B.C.: New Society Publishers, 2002. Print.

Healy, Jane M. *Endangered Minds: Why Children Don't Think and What We Can Do About It*. New York, NY: Simon & Schuster, 1990. Print.

Herr, Norman. "Television & Health." *www.csun.edu*. Internet Resources to Accompany the Sourcebook for Teaching Science, n.d. Web. 11 March 2015

"How TV Affects Your Child." *Kidshealth.org*. Nemours, n.d. Web. 11 March 2015.

Nagin, Carl and The National Writing Project. *Because Writing Matters*. San Fransisco, CA: John Wiley & Sons, Inc., 2006. Print.

Sanchez, Claudio. "College Board 'Concerned' About Low SAT Scores." *npr.org*. National Public Radio, 26 Sep 2013. Web. 24 Sep 2014.

Seligman, Martin E. P., Ph. D. *Learned Optimism: How to Change Your Mind and Your Life*. New York, NY: Free Press, 1998. Print.

Made in the USA
San Bernardino, CA
18 April 2015